Cat Behavior

BY MARIE PEARSON

An Imprint of Abdo Publishing
abdobooks.com

abdobooks.com

Published by Abdo Publishing, a division of ABDO, PO Box 398166, Minneapolis, Minnesota 55439.

Printed in the United States of America, North Mankato, Minnesota.
052023
092023

THIS BOOK CONTAINS
RECYCLED MATERIALS

Cover Photo: Ian McGlasham/Shutterstock Images
Interior Photos: Shutterstock Images, 4–5, 12–13, 17, 20–21, 28, 29; Africa Studio/Shutterstock Images, 7; LightField Studios/Shutterstock Images, 8; Wavebreak Media/Shutterstock Images, 9; Andriy Blokhin/Shutterstock Images, 10; Jaromir Chalabala/Shutterstock Images, 14; Elena Rozhenok/Shutterstock Images, 16; Anna Krivitskaya/Shutterstock Images, 18; Alevtina Gorskaya/Shutterstock Images, 23; Sozina Kseniia/Shutterstock Images, 24; Alexander Dubrovsky/Shutterstock Images, 26

Editor: Mary Shaw
Series Designer: Katharine Hale

Library of Congress Control Number: 2022949077

Publisher's Cataloging-in-Publication Data

Names: Pearson, Marie, author.
Title: Cat behavior / by Marie Pearson
Description: Minneapolis, Minnesota: Abdo Publishing Company, 2024 | Series: Animal behavior | Includes online resources and index.
Identifiers: ISBN 9781098291013 (lib. bdg.) | ISBN 9781098277192 (ebook)
Subjects: LCSH: Cats--Behavior--Juvenile literature. | Cats--Juvenile literature. | Mammalogy--Juvenile literature.
Classification: DDC 591.51--dc23

CONTENTS

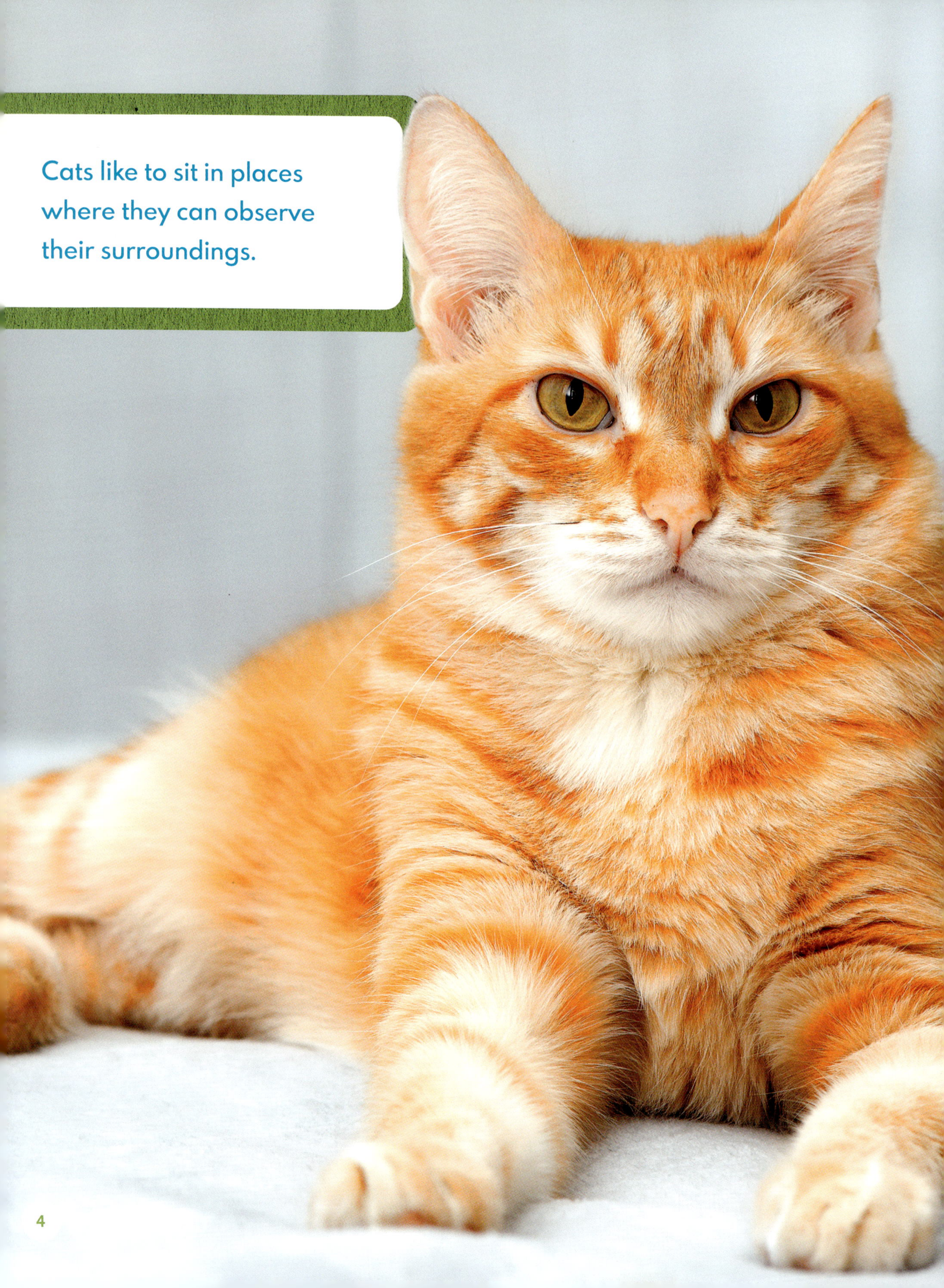

Cats like to sit in places where they can observe their surroundings.

CHAPTER 1

Making Friends

Luke carried his sleeping bag and backpack into his friend DeShawn's room. They were having a sleepover. Luke dropped his things on the floor. Then he noticed the orange cat sitting on the bed.

"You have a cat!" Luke said as he went over to the bed. He started rubbing the cat's belly like his dog always enjoyed. Instead of wagging its tail like his dog usually did, the cat flattened its ears and leaped off the bed to hide in DeShawn's closet. Luke felt bad that the cat didn't want to play with him.

Petting Cats

People should pet cats gently with an open hand. Most cats do not like to be poked or have their fur grabbed. Cats usually prefer being petted on the head, neck, and back. They often dislike being petted on the face, belly, paws, or tail.

When a cat is feeling nervous, it may find somewhere to hide.

DeShawn said, "Her name is Ruby. Just ignore her for a while. When she comes up to you, you can pet her. She likes gentle petting on her back."

When a cat is ready for attention, it may want to be petted.

Later that evening, Luke and DeShawn were watching a movie. Ruby came over to Luke and sniffed his feet. Luke let her sniff a bit. Then he gently stroked her back a couple of times. Ruby rubbed his leg. DeShawn said, “See, she likes you! You just have to know how she wants to hang out.”

Approaching someone is one way a cat may show that it feels comfortable and safe.

A cat will use its sense of smell to learn about a new environment or person.

Learning Cat Behavior

People rely mostly on speech to communicate. But cats are different. They use mainly body language to share how they are feeling. They also use sound and smell.

Cats can show many emotions. They can show happiness. They can also show fear. If people know what cats are saying, both people and cats have happier interactions. When a person responds to what a cat is saying, that helps the cat trust the person more.

Explore Online

Visit the website below. Does it give any new information about cat behavior that wasn't in Chapter One?

Why Do Cats Rub Round Their Owners' Legs?

abdocorelibrary.com/cat-behavior

Cats can use body language to communicate with each other.

CHAPTER 2

Cat to Cat

Cats need to be able to show how they feel to other cats. They do this with their behavior. Cats have many ways to show their feelings.

A happy, relaxed cat will blink slowly. The cat might purr. It may turn its head away.

A cat may purr to show that it is feeling happy.

This is a sign it feels safe. Cats greet each other by touching noses. They rub their heads on each other as a sign of **affection**. Comfortable cats knead. This is when a cat seems to massage a soft surface, such as a blanket or a lap, with its front paws. Cats may purr when kneading.

A cat may roll on its back to start playing. Playful cats will wrestle and gently bite and swat. The cats typically won't get hurt, even though it looks rough. Their ears will be held naturally, and they won't extend their claws. Cats are typically quiet when they play.

Scent Communication

Cats release scents through parts of the body including the paws, cheeks, forehead, and tail. They spread these scents by scratching or rubbing items. Their urine also has scents that the cats spread by spraying. All these scents can be used to mark territory.

When a cat is scared, its pupils might become big and round.

Stress and Aggression

Cats who are stressed or fearful may try to hide. They may crouch down to look small. Their **pupils** will be wider than normal. A stressed cat might hold its tail against its body. The ears and whiskers will flatten back. A very fearful cat will hiss, and its fur will puff out. It may also become aggressive.

Comparing Emotions

Trusting "I trust you!"		Relaxed, exposing belly
Relaxed "I'm friendly!"		Relaxed posture, mouth closed, tail held upright
Nervous "I'm worried and unsure."		Ears turned sideways, body tense, tail low
Scared "Please leave me alone."		Crouching or lying down, head low, tail tucked tightly, large pupils
Angry "Stay away!"		Body flattened, ears drawn back, hissing or growling

Cats have many ways of showing how they feel. Body language is one of the main ways they do this.

Flattening their ears is one way that cats show aggression.

Aggressive cats have very large pupils. Their ears will flatten back, but the whiskers will be to the side. The back is arched, and the tail is held high. An aggressive cat will stare without blinking. It will growl. Eventually, aggressive cats might bite or scratch.

Primary Source

John Bradshaw is the author of *Cat Sense: How the New Feline Science Can Make You a Better Friend to Your Pet*. He said this about cat behavior:

> I think cats show, by their behavior, even if it's a bit more **subtle** than a dog's, that they really are fond of their owners.

Source: John Bradshaw. "What's Mittens Thinking? Make 'Sense' of Your Cat's Behavior." *NPR*, 5 Sept. 2013, npr.org. Accessed 15 Nov. 2022.

Point of View

What is the author's point of view on this topic? What is your point of view? Write a short essay about how they are similar and different.

Changes in a cat's behavior may be a sign that it needs to visit the vet.

CHAPTER 3

Body Language and Care

Knowing how cats are feeling can help people care for them. Cats don't always purr when happy. Sometimes they purr if they are feeling ill. Sick cats will have less energy than usual. They might **groom** themselves less or groom too much.

They may also eat or drink less. They could also eat or drink more, and they might stop using the litter box. Owners should watch for changes in behavior and take their cats to the vet if necessary.

Behavior Issues

Some cat behaviors, such as scratching furniture, can make owners upset.

Why Cats Meow

Kittens meow to their mothers. Adult cats rarely meow to other cats. But they do it a lot to people. This is because people respond to and reward meows with attention. If people ignore meowing, the cats stop doing it.

Giving a cat places to play, climb, and scratch can help it stay active.

Scratching is a natural behavior. Owners need to give their cats many things that are OK to scratch and train the cats to use them.

Bored cats might groom or eat too much. They may not seem interested in much around them. Owners can make their cats happier by giving them different toys and playing with the cats. People can set up climbing and scratching spots and places for cats to lie next to windows.

A cat may react with biting or scratching if it does not want to be petted.

Aggression

If a cat is being aggressive, people should give it space. Even if the cat is just flicking its tail and has its ears back, it should be left alone. It is saying it doesn't feel safe.

Owners should take an aggressive cat to the vet and make sure it isn't sick. They should try to find out what is making the cat aggressive. Then they can avoid exposing the cat to this **situation**. Owners can use treats to reward the cat for calm, friendly behavior.

Some cats suddenly become aggressive when being petted. This might be because the cats are **overstimulated**, but scientists aren't sure. People can try petting cats for just short periods. They can give cats treats while being petted to make it a good experience. They should stop anytime the cat starts showing signs of aggression.

A trusting cat will greet people by sniffing their hands or faces.

Building Trust

Cats trust people who listen when the cats show they aren't comfortable. If a cat walks away, it wants space. A person should not follow it.

Instead, people should let cats come to them, and they should get down to the cat's level.

Cats often like people who are quiet and sit still. These are signals to cats that these people are safe, and cats will often move close to them. When people understand a cat's behavior, the cats and humans have a better relationship.

Further Evidence

Look at the website below. Does it give any new evidence to support Chapter Three?

Pet Cats

abdocorelibrary.com/cat-behavior

Body Language

Happy and Relaxed

Scared

Glossary

affection
showing care toward a person or animal

groom
to lick the fur with the tongue

overstimulated
had too much sensory interaction from things like noise, touch, or play

pupils
the dark centers of the eyes

situation
a certain combination of location, objects, and sometimes events

subtle
not obvious

Online Resources

To learn more about cat behavior, visit our free resource websites below.

Visit **abdocorelibrary.com** or scan this QR code for free Common Core resources for teachers and students, including vetted activities, multimedia, and booklinks, for deeper subject comprehension.

Visit **abdobooklinks.com** or scan this QR code for free additional online weblinks for further learning. These links are routinely monitored and updated to provide the most current information available.

Learn More

Jenner, Caryn. *Cats and Kittens*. DK, 2020.

MacMillan, Kathy. *Cats*. Abdo, 2023.

Osborne, Mary Pope, and Jenny Laird. *Snow Leopards and Other Wild Cats*. Random House, 2022.

Index

About the Author

Marie Pearson is a children's book author and editor. She spends her free time learning about animal behavior and training. She taught a cat she lived with several tricks, including to wave and lie down.